ELLEN PHELAN

FROM THE LIVES OF DOLLS

UNIVERSITY GALLERY, FINE ARTS CENTER,
UNIVERSITY OF MASSACHUSETTS AT AMHERST

SAIDYE BRONFMAN CENTRE,
MONTREAL

THE CONTEMPORARY MUSEUM,
HONOLULU

This publication was prepared in conjunction with the exhibition *Ellen Phelan: From the Lives of Dolls*, organized by the University Gallery of the University of Massachusetts at Amherst. Guest-curated by Marge Goldwater, the exhibition was presented at the University Gallery from November 7 through December 18, 1992, at the Saidye Bronfman Centre, Montreal, from February 17 through March 17, 1993, and at The Contemporary Museum, Honolulu, from April 6 through May 30, 1993.

The exhibition and publication were made possible by The Douglas S. Cramer Foundation and the Massachusetts Cultural Council. The UMass Arts Council, the University Alumni Association, and the Friends of the Fine Arts Center support the University Gallery's programming.

ISBN 0-929597-02-8 Library of Congress Number: 92-82616

Catalogue design by Jim Burke, University Design and Production Services

This document was created on a Macintosh IICX with Linotronic 300 processing. This publication was printed in an edition of 2000 by Excelsior Printing, North Adams, Massachusetts.

UNIVERSITY GALLERY STAFF
Betsy Siersma, Director
Regina Coppola, Curator
Jennifer Lind, Registrar
Craig Allaben, Gallery Manager
Justin Griswold, Preparator
Donna Swist, Secretary
David Aaronoff, Vanessa Kam, Interns

ADVISORY BOARD
Carl Belz, Hanlyn Davies, Avital Sagalyn, Frederick C. Tillis

Title page: *Artist's Westport studio, 1992*
Photograph: Ken Burris

PHOTOGRAPHY CREDITS
Dirk Bakker: 6 below, 18 below, 25
Ken Burris: 19, 22
Geoffrey Clements: 9
Barry Kahn: 14
Quiriconi-Tropea: 11
Zindman-Fremont: 6 above, 12, 15-17, 18 above, 20, 21, 23, 26-29,

LENDERS TO THE EXHIBITION
Asher/Faure
Ross Bleckner
Dr. Jack E. Chachkes
Freddy and Candy DeMann
Ann Ehrenkrantz
Bruce and Judith Eissner
Irwin and Judith Elson
Eric Fischl
Mr. and Mrs. Peter Frank
Susanne Feld Hilberry and Richard Kandarian
Susanne Hilberry Gallery
Raymond J. Learsy
Mr. and Mrs. Eric Lieber
Dr. and Mrs. Gordon M. Moss
Elizabeth Murray
Mr. and Mrs. John O'Neill
Michael and Judy Ovitz
Ellen Phelan
Jean C. Pigozzi
Joel Shapiro
Jeffrey Slatkin
Barbara Toll
Barbara Toll Fine Arts
Dr. and Mrs. Martin Weissman
David Wirtz
Irene Worth
H. David Zucca
Three Private Collections

FOREWORD

The idea to organize an exhibition of Ellen Phelan's drawings and paintings was introduced to us over two years ago by Marge Goldwater, who was, at the time, an independent curator in New York. We agreed that Ellen's work deserved the attention of a major exhibition, in particular her drawings of dolls, a subject matter that has interested her since the late 1970s, and the recent paintings that are based on that same imagery. Ellen's collection of dolls—a detail of which is pictured facing the title page—provided the inspiration for her evocative expressions that reveal the secret places of human psychology and emotions. Sentimental or frightening, sad or ridiculous, Ellen's images convey the humor and vulnerability of being alive. Atmospheres which infused childhood play with dolls are here rendered with the talent of a masterful artist and the experiences of a grown woman. The University Gallery is pleased to present the first major exhibition of Ellen Phelan's doll imagery which provides the comparative context within which to assess this increasingly important aspect of her art.

Many individuals have contributed to the success of the exhibition and the accompanying catalogue. I would like to extend our appreciation to Marge Goldwater for her many efforts that resulted in this thoughtful exhibition. Richard Armstrong and Peter Schjeldahl have contributed essays for the exhibition catalogue that provide important insights into Ellen's work. To all three we express our warmest appreciation. The exhibition and catalogue have been organized by the University Gallery's dedicated staff. Special thanks must be given to Jennifer Lind, Registrar, who deftly handled the complicated shipping arrangements, and carefully prepared the catalogue checklist, and the artist's biography and bibliography. From the University's Design and Production Services, our thanks go to Jim Burke for his catalogue design that beautifully reflects the essence of the artist's work.

We are grateful to The Douglas S. Cramer Foundation and the Massachusetts Cultural Council, whose support has made the exhibition and catalogue possible. The UMass Arts Council and the University Alumni Association continue to support the University Gallery's exhibition program. The exhibition would not have been possible without the help of Barbara Toll Fine Arts in New York, the Susanne Hilberry Gallery in Birmingham, Michigan, and Asher/Faure in Los Angeles. Many thanks are due to Barbara Toll and Frank Lemann, Susanne Hilberry and Sandra Schemske, and Pat Faure for their assistance with shipping, photography, and numerous other important details. We are pleased that the exhibition will be shared with the Saidye Bronfman Centre, Montreal and The Contemporary Museum, Honolulu. Our thanks go to Regine Basha and Jay Jensen. Finally, to the collectors who have so graciously agreed to lend their work to the exhibition, we extend our sincere appreciation.

Betsy Siersma, Director

II. *Baby and Pierre*, 1985

I. *Applause*, 1985

PREFACE

Ellen Phelan's art has always been at odds with prevailing fashions. In the 1970s it was abstract when excitement in the art world began to center on new figuration. Some years later her work became representational just as abstraction was regaining prominence. Even as contemporary landscape painting developed a certain vogue in the late 1980s, Phelan's work remained unfashionable because her non-conceptual approach to the subject was old-fashioned. It did not seem surprising, therefore, when in 1984 a curious and out-of-sync choice of subject matter–dolls–began to appear in her work.

The paintings and works on paper in this exhibition, all based on doll images, proceeded in the same fashion as Phelan's landscapes (a theme that continues to engage her). Just as the landscapes began as plein-air studies on paper, the doll imagery was also worked up directly from the subject–dolls set up in front of the artist. The subsequent paintings are all based on specific works on paper, an approach that parallels her current working method vis à vis landscape, as Richard Armstrong describes more fully in the essay that follows.

For many years Phelan did not consider doing paintings based on the dolls. But this newest body of work–

fourteen paintings thus far, of which eleven are included in the present exhibition–makes abundantly clear that the figurative work is not an inexplicable detour from the landscape work but a complement to it. The exhibition, which has had a long gestation period, changed its focus with the appearance of the doll paintings. They inspired us to concentrate exclusively on the figurative work, to bring together a larger number of the drawings than originally planned, and to look at them in relation to the wonderful new paintings that emerged.

These psychologically charged images occupy an interesting midpoint between still life and figure painting while roving between seeming obviousness and maddening obscurity. They avoid the danger common to figurative art of being too illustrational, just as Phelan's abstract work managed to avoid the problem of being overly decorative. Neither politically correct nor incorrect, they are stubbornly honest. Economical in their means, they are rich in results.

Marge Goldwater

ELLEN PHELAN TO DATE

by Richard Armstrong

Ellen Phelan's conversion from gestural abstraction to symbolic representation rehearses the story of her generation of painters: artists who came of age around 1975 and began working in the formidable and intellectually rigid shadow of Minimalism—a rational and highly articulated system that fostered comparably intellectual work. In spirit and in aspiration, Phelan and her peers were younger kin to the so-called Postminimalists, sculptors such as Eva Hesse, Bruce Nauman, Barry Le Va, Richard Tuttle, and Richard Serra, who shared antiformalist sentiments that led them to exalt the idiosyncrasies of materials and processes. What these new sculptors shared with the Minimalists was an ingrained prejudice against figurative art, tempered by a sense of scale and a common rhetoric that insisted on the body as measure and psychic arbiter. Phelan, along with Elizabeth Murray and Susan Rothenberg, absorbed this *Zeitgeist* of body-centrism, even as they turned to representational imagery: Rothenberg from the beginning of her career, Murray around 1980, and Phelan five years later. Their work is redolent with specific, figurative images that profoundly contradict the universalist fields of both Minimalism and Postminimalism. In different ways and through varying means, all three artists have sought to reinvest painting with the force of metaphor derived from autobiography.

A Detroit native, Phelan had studied painting at Wayne State University through the 1960s. She respected the work of and felt an affinity for the realist Robert Wilbert, who in turn admired his young student's skills—especially as a draftsman. The arrival in 1967 of Sam Wagstaff, curator of contemporary art at The Detroit Institute of Arts (DIA), galvanized the area's interesting

artists, most of whom worked in studios on or near Cass Avenue in midtown Detroit. In 1971 they banded together to open a cooperative showplace, the Willis Gallery. Soon the press began to speak of a "Cass Corridor style," although the work in question shared little more than a taste for expressionist reconfigurations of urban detritus. The recognition their work garnered reflected the artists' intense commitment to their mode of expression in their activity and the strong support of the well-connected Wagstaff. One observer characterized their cumulative effort as "the presence of a naked will to style, the conviction of young artists that they could make art out of sheer desire to be artists." [1]

In 1969, troubled by what she felt was an inability to invent convincing two-dimensional abstract forms, Phelan had begun making the space of painting literal. In her first forays into three dimensions she cut and folded unstretched canvas into zig-zag shapes painted on all sides with different colors to signal planar shifts. In subsequent wall-bound process pieces, she used torn, painted, unstretched canvas as an eccentric armature for somberly colored heraldic shapes or tied grids. From soft works there evolved a series of shallow reliefs, wood chairs, and ladders wrapped in cloth. By 1972 Phelan had begun a series that occupied her for three years of freestanding open or partially open fan shapes, built to the scale of her body. Made of canvas attached to a wooden armature visible from one side, the monochromatic fans, though sometimes stiffened with plaster, were self-supporting paintings on eccentrically rounded canvases.

Phelan's empirical interest in process accelerated in early 1972 as she came to know such artists as Elizabeth

Untitled (standing circle), 1972
4' x 4' x 6"
Lathe, Paris-craft, plaster, pigment and tar
Collection of the artist

Murray, Jennifer Bartlett, Mike Goldberg, George Trakas, and particularly Jackie Winsor, whom she assisted in making a piece on site for a group show at the DIA.

With encouragement from these artists, Phelan moved to New York in 1973, seeking a more critical and sophisticated milieu in which to work–one that would be more accepting of a woman artist than the Detroit scene. Shortly after her arrival she met the sculptor Joel Shapiro; five years later they married.

Some of Phelan's fans were included in a group show at Paula Cooper Gallery in 1975, while others were featured at a solo show at Artists Space the same month. The supportive reception for the fans at Paula Cooper was typical of the gallery's timely reaction to a new, broadly manifested aesthetic, exemplified by the work of Murray, Shapiro, Winsor, Bartlett, and Jonathan Borofsky. Phelan's work, by comparison to theirs or even to that of her contemporaries in Detroit, looked restrained, lushly made, and slightly historical. Then as now, Phelan comfortably

proclaimed stylistic antecedents—she has always seemed to situate herself within a lineage.

At the same time other artists (and friends of Phelan), such as Marilyn Lenkowsky and Ron Gorchov, were similarly experimenting with eccentrically shaped supports for their painting. Their work was included in the 1975 Whitney Museum Biennial—a show which, in its wide-ranging inclusiveness, highlighted many of the incipient ideas that would dominate art for the next five years. Like Phelan, these artists sought a means to revive painting in the face of the relentlessly intellectual assault of the Conceptualists and the more programmatic Minimalists.

Although the fans had been well received in 1975, their monochromism had begun to dissatisfy Phelan. In a two-artist show at Paula Cooper in 1976 she showed attenuated works that resembled sails, their backs left raw, their fronts painted two colors to indicate structural differences in their surfaces. As she later recalled, "At this point I took my work more abstract. I began making work with more than one plane, making each plane a different color. I spent a lot of time questioning the painting support—first, the rectangle, and second, the stretcher bars—the relationship of color to form, how to justify using two colors, and dealing with that by altering the shapes of the support."[2]

Around 1976 she adopted a new three-dimensional format for her painted sculptures. On wooden, splayed U-shaped structures she attached a horizontal picture plane at about midpoint on the seven-foot-high support. These small wooden rectangles reasserted the construct's essential frontality; though she painted only the face, Phelan situated a horizon physically and tonally–in fact, a picture on an exaggerated vertical. These pieces were technically a fusion of two- and three-dimensional strategies, while metaphorically they alluded both to landscape and the figure. In converting the eccentric shapes and formal irregularities of the fans to rigid and geometricized structures, Phelan assumed new freedoms with color. Her restrained palette increased to a full chromatic range, and she exploited the uniform, planar surfaces to juxtapose

Untitled, 1978
Oil on plywood
84" x 18 ¹/₂" x 8 ¹/₂"
Private Collection

This group of gouache drawings foretold Phelan's return to realism. In the following two years, much of which she spent in Los Angeles while teaching at nearby CalArts, she painted on L-shaped metal plates. Using an emphatically gestural style, derived from her way of painting fans, she tried out a variety of strokes, erasures, and revisions, working wet on wet, to create the units of these four-part compositions. Configuring the L's into larger open squares, cruciforms, H-shapes, pinwheels, and even swastikas, Phelan distinguished, by color and motion, one component from another. Intended originally to be composed of interchangeable parts, each of the assembled wholes projected an integrated, rigorously non-objective uniqueness. Further, they were an extended effort to use color and gesture freely, released from the necessities of planar description. The persuasive powers of illusionist painting were by now obvious to her.

The milky, tenebrous imagery Phelan conjured of the monochromatic gouache fed her concurrent and still abstract painting. The contradiction between materiality and illusion lent these works a tautness that was compounded by the centralized tension inferred in their mostly centripetal force. This two-dimensional tension between image and object evolved naturally from the fans and her earlier torn-canvas pieces and remains an abiding concern. In aluminum plate pictures such as *The Islands* (1980-81), Phelan nominates place as her work's subject, however generalized its gestural rendition. In the L-shaped panels, she fragmented and rearranged passages, insisting on a flattened, ultimately abstracted space that was foreign to the window-on-the-world panorama of her drawings. How to bring the two bodies of her work into alignment occupied Phelan throughout the first half of the 1980s. "Because the drawings were black-and-white, they would get me to the bones of a situation. Then I would try to make paintings that reminded me of the light and color, and of the experience of being in the space."[3] Exposing the fictional illusionism of her paintings while continuing her longtime consideration of shape and support, she physically altered the picture plane, thus demonstrating

unlikely but complementary colors—dominated by blues and greens—into evocative combinations. These pieces slowly, empirically led Phelan back to the wall, as she became more and more challenged by the inherent possibilities of painting.

During a summer stay at a lake in the Adirondacks in 1976, Phelan began again working representationally on paper. Her drawings of the previous seven years had been a physical extension of her concern for process and literal space: they had been cut, folded, torn, and collaged. Now she turned to black gouache on stretched paper for plein-air drawings in which she recorded the lake and forest she saw daily.

The Islands, 1980-81
Oil on aluminum
48" x 96"
Private Collection

the paintings' two-dimensional constraints: notched edges, rectangular cuts, open and gauze-covered holes undeniably revealed the quantifiably shallow space behind the inferred, atmospheric depths of her gestures.

Her imagery also evolved. While the gouaches fed Phelan's growing appetite for locatable subject, the formal genesis of her paintings was inspired by classical sources— such as Watteau, Corot, and Turner. Freely adapting their more representational works to her charged, wet-into-wet treatments, she sought to replicate the luminosities particular to each artist. Her titles from this period acknowledged many of these historical references, just as her geometric incisions and removals located, by their very excision, critical passages in the prototypes. While the massing and atmospheric tonalities of her paintings resembled their mostly nineteenth-century models, she consistently emptied her work of figurative subject matter. Absence became a *de facto* theme–not only through its

literal manifestation–but also in Phelan's consistent editing out of the human presences that are common in her sources. Hers were depopulated paintings, removed from any narrative functions, oriented to formalist concerns.

Around 1988, Phelan began to consider her works on paper partly as suitable starting points for paintings, "It's a great pleasure to have an image to start from. The drawing is essentially a hieroglyph and becomes a prod to memory– at a certain point when I'm working on a painting, I remember exactly what I was looking at, and in that peculiar moment I can, in a sense, reinhabit the image." [4] By responding to her own reactions to nature, rather than to a venerated symbol of romantic naturalism, Phelan's paintings gained the authority of observation. Variations on empirical data, they signaled her increasing desire to work with what was in front of her, to concretize what was real, at hand, and of the present.

11

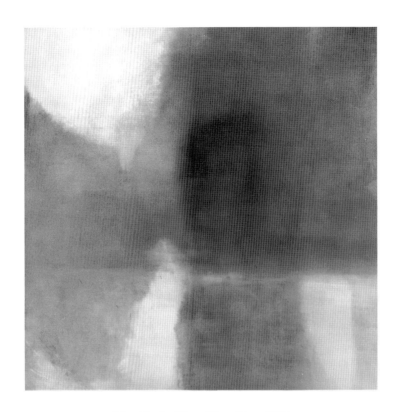

Island in the River–River Test, 1989
Oil on linen
51 ¹/₄" x 45 ⁵/₈"
Collection The Brooklyn Museum 1991.11
Gift of Edward A. Bragaline, by exchange

What was at hand were scores of finished gouache and watercolor landscape drawings from Ireland, Norway, Belize, and Mexico; others were the result of summers spent on eastern Long Island or, after 1985, of extended stays at a house in the pine woods ashore Lake Champlain. Her lakeside studio, formerly a ballroom atop a boathouse, affords Phelan great vistas up and down the lake and sustained natural light.

With the decision to work with a known specific image, Phelan's painting techniques became more subdued. The emphatically gestural strokes of the previous years assumed less importance to Phelan when she was working from her own grisaille drawings. The paintings, physically magnified renderings of the drawings, also took on their muted coloration. So ethereally simple are paintings such as *Meadow Hampshire-Storm: Dark Low Clouds* (1989) and *Island in the River–River Test* (1989) that they constitute an apogee of Whistlerian hazy luminescence. Utterly uninhabited and idyllic, Phelan's subjects had taken her about as far away from the quotidian as possible. This otherworldliness, a small universe of milky light and blurred shadows, remains her stage today.

Beginning in 1985, Phelan further satisfied her realist tendencies, which date back to her training as a student, with a series of works on paper depicting dolls. Once again, by media, scale, and image she was pursuing two kinds of work simultaneously. Like the landscapes, the dolls were initially confined to black gouache on paper. For her, they symbolized a rich matrix of still life and portraiture possibilities.

12

Phelan, hailing from a family of self-proclaimed pack rats, had originally shipped her childhood collection of dolls to New York for her stepdaughter to enjoy, adding the occasional yard sale or thrift shop find over the years. Thus her own Madame Alexander dolls, fine ladies all, were supplemented by a company of characters with which she could devise setups ripe with psychological and narrative possibilities. Her first forays, such as *Applause* (1985), typically featured only one or two characters rendered in some detail, centered on the page in dramatic poses. Here were the good little girls, performing various roles for adult approval. A series of brides, diaphanous in watercolor, were next, followed by an array of misfits, including such cultural oddities as a humanized beer logo–the first of an expanding subspecies of drinking mascots, all male. Phelan had quickly embraced a wide range of dolls and playthings along with their implied actions and potential combinations and recombinations. Although females–mothers, daughters, sisters, wives, vixens (even coy kitties)–predominate, they often coexist with male counterparts in a surrogate and grown-up world. "When you play with dolls, they are animated by the projection of imagination. As opposed to the material projected by a child, the material I was projecting was adult. It really had to do with emotional relationships between men and women, mothers and daughters, gender definition and how it comes about, the female sense of the self." [5]

In this newly apparent quest for metaphoric identity, Phelan's trajectory as an artist intersects with that of peers such as Murray and Rothenberg. The still life and the schematized figures that dominate Murray's fractured and torqued canvases testify to her continuing attention to a Cubism filtered through Miro, while Rothenberg's dry enigmatic linear figures descend from Giacometti's drawings. The antecedents for Phelan's work seem twofold, and distinctly more American: Edwin Dickinson's *premier coup* paintings–landscapes and portraits, completed in a few hours of intense concentration and highly gestural bravura. Describing these works in words well suited to Phelan's version of realism, Dickinson often said, "The

general would never come from the particular, but the particular was included in the general." But in her use of closely observed setups, Phelan's doll drawings and paintings recall Walter Murch's luminous icons of the ordinary. Although best known for his Chardinesque renderings of small machinery, Murch also worked from nature and, around 1965, with dolls themselves. As with Phelan's recent body of work, he seems to have been attracted to commonplace talismans, subjects made rich by human use. Like Murch, Phelan's miraculous transformations use light, deft rendering to impart significance. From modest means, in a so-called "academic" way, each conjures symbols that speak to its moment. For if Murch's embrace of the banal has about it a sense of longing for a simpler past, Phelan's doll works address the overwhelming urgency of feminism in contemporary art. In the past year Phelan has begun to make large paintings from the doll drawings, paintings in which Phelan's revelatory intent is hardly questionable. As with Murray and Rothenberg, the allusions in Phelan's works are graphically real, overtly emotional, and demonstratively titled: *Applause, A Shock (Oh-Oh), Rejecting Mother, Spectre of Age, The Kiss: Revenge,* and *Reconciliation,* among them. Her themes in works such as these are autobiographical: she has even cited the drawings *Down Life's Highway* and *Self as Elf* as surrogate self-portraits with Shapiro, while the brides, in their various degrees of ambivalence, are modelled on the female figurine that was on her own wedding cake.

The new tension in Phelan's work is one of subject and setting. She addresses, even re-creates, in miniature, socially charged situations in an unabashedly romantic way. In the series of *Blond White Woman* drawings, for instance, Phelan scrutinizes a media icon of the 1970s, Farrah Fawcett, seeing in her doll likeness the embodiment of a host of male (and, by transference, female) fantasies fueled by desire. The disembodied corporeality of de Kooning's *Women* of the early 1950s are forebears of Phelan's forlorn, emaciated, and eerily distant figures.

In fact, an unmistakable sense of memorial pervades nearly all these drawings, the gauzy, atmospheric haze of gouache rendering them visually distant, their figures stranded in time. In the more recent paintings, which are enlargements and reconstructions of the drawings, Phelan's time-honed painting skills make the oil medium perfectly congruent with the drawn sources in gouache. Abstract and shadowy grounds carry equal weight with the object– mute figures temporarily illuminated in a roiling atmosphere of the unspoken. Phelan has joined gestural abstraction with symbolic representation in a format that comfortably carries both relevance and a sense of transcendence. With these dolls she has found inhabitants for her surrogate world, an illusion of paint, hand, and fantasy. As

Camus once noted, the whole of a person's artistic expression is the attempt to recapture through art those two or three images in whose presence his soul first opened. It seems Phelan has found her image.

1. Robert Pincus-Witten, "Detroit Notes: Islands in the Blight," *Arts Magazine*, 52 (June 1978), p. 138.

2. Margaret Moorman, "Ellen Phelan: Shapechanger," *Art News*, 91 (February 1992), p. 111.

3. Ibid., p. 112.

4. Ibid.

5. Gerrit Henry, "Ellen Phelan: The Interpretation of Dolls," *The Print Collector's Newsletter*, 19 (May-June 1988), p. 52.

New York City studio, 1981

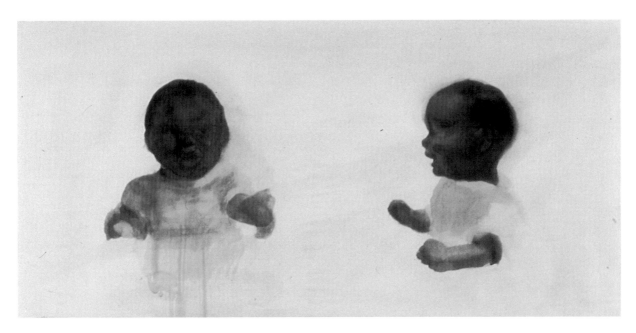

XVIII. *Mug Shot*, 1987

XLI. *War: Sailor and Barmaid*, 1991

XXXVII. *Rehearsal*, 1991

XIX. *Traveling Costume*, 1987

XLV. *Rehearsal*, 1991

X. *Rejecting Mother*, 1986

XLVI. *Rejecting Mother*, 1991

L. *The Beautiful Mother*, 1992

XL. *The Kiss: Revenge*, 1991

LI. *The Kiss: Betrayal*, 1992

LII. *Street Scene: Memory of Detroit (for Joyce Carol Oates)*, 1992

XLIV. *Overheard: The Conversation*, 1991

DOLLNESS: ELLEN PHELAN'S DOLL DRAWINGS

by Peter Schjeldahl

It was nighttime in Los Angeles and my little daughter was crying for her baby doll. Had we left it at the Avis office where earlier we rented a car? I phoned, and, yes, they had it. Whew! Returning there in a hurry, I rushed to the counter and blurted, "I've come to pick up a doll."

"Well," one of several young women behind the counter said frostily, "you have come to the wrong place!"

Carefully made up in her neat uniform with the "We Try Harder" button, she did look sort of doll-like, come to think of it, even as she glared at me (flabbergasted-man doll) with outraged rectitude. It was so funny I couldn't laugh.

Remembering that incident helps me think about Ellen Phelan's elegant and treacherous watercolors and gouaches of dolls–elegant in technique and form, an ongoing virtuosic *tour de force*, and treacherous in content. She started making them in the late 1970s as gifts for friends and as breaks from her abstract and landscape painting. In the mid-1980s they got out of hand. There are over a hundred of them now, an expanding doll cosmos. Phelan has discovered in her responsiveness to dolls, made communicable by graphic skills equal to any nuance, a royal road to her own and everybody else's unconscious.

The work is consistently comic and just as consistently all but impossible to laugh at, because to get her jokes is to be trapped in them. Proper viewers of Phelan's doll drawings must be willing to regard themselves, among other people, in a light at once tender and ridiculous. I will try to follow my own advice here in my role of art-critic doll.

Life imitating a cartoon, my standoff with the Avis person was a moment of exquisite misunderstanding quite appropriately involving a double entendre of "doll." Dolls are materialized exquisite misunderstandings. They are dead things generating delusions of life. They are wish-fulfilling travesties meant to stir day-dreamy play. Just how various and subtle the field of that play might be, and above all how laced with specifiable ambivalences, I think I never suspected until encountering Phelan's repertoire, but I always knew dolls are often derisive and often sentimental.

Common speech conveys the negative and positive feeling tones we invest in dolls. The Avis woman heard herself derided as a "doll" in the sense of plaything, less than fully human. But she would hardly mind a fellow worker, for instance, saying of her, "She's a doll," suggesting superhuman amiability. Here we have a major dialectic of dolls–caricature versus idealization–that whipsaws through Phelan's drawings, helping to explain the unsettling gravity of what looks at first glance, delightfully, like a toyshop come to life. Eventually one starts to suspect that Phelan's toys are disguised avatars of Goya's *dramatis personae*, with Edvard Munch supervising *mise en scène* and James Ensor cackling in the orchestra pit.

Phelan's scariest drawings are those in which idealizing dolls flip over into caricature, as in her *Blonde White Woman* series based on a Farrah Fawcett item radiating fantasies of long-haired, long-necked, pretty-woman perfection. Nudged by Phelan's watercolor brush, the image generates a kaleidoscopic rogues gallery of hyperfeminine monsters, each as instantly familiar as a remembered unfavorite aunt or the latest filthy-rich WASPette in the gossip columns. Conversely, among the most moving of Phelan's pictures are those that render dolls originally caricatural–especially blacks reeking of the

XXXIII. *Blonde White Woman #9*, 1991

old vicious Jim Crow condescension–with an intensity of feeling that hovers between adoration and sorrow, seeking in objects of scorn a solidarity with the absolutely human. Phelan is on dangerous ground with these drawings. On what other sort of ground should an artist wish to be?

With such exceptions as the Farrah Fawcett doll and an obscene and pathetic cameo appearance of *Bud Man,* Phelan prefers relatively antique dolls, whose remoteness from present fashion affords a strangeness congenial to the imagination. She eschews strangeness-proof contemporary engines of gender indoctrination like Barbie and G.I. Joe. Socially conscientious rather than politically correct, Phelan is alert to stereotypes but leaves obvious targets and bloodless "criticality" to others. She seems less interested in "gender issues," for instance, than in what used to be called more reverberantly the battle of the sexes.

In her choice of models, Phelan emphasizes essential dollness, the quality of dolls addressed both to the eye and the hand: to be gazed upon, to be played with. Her images thus differ from other recent toy-based art, such as the

coldly spectacular figurines of Jeff Koons and the touchy-feely stuffed creatures of Mike Kelley. If she shares anything with those contemporaries, it may be fascination with the unguardedness of our culture when it comes to toys, letting so much embarrassing information hang out in plain view.

Embarrassment is like an atmosphere, a sticky humidity, in the world of Phelan's dolls, which are helpless to keep secrets. When sentimental, like the brides and singers, they are desperately so, abjectly and plungingly sentimental. They are immolated in sentimentality like moths in a flame. The effect is sadness, with an upbeat of compassion. When derisory, like the drunks and some of the clowns, they are manically derisory, falling all over themselves to participate in their own humiliation. The effect is, again, sadness with an upbeat. A willingness to be ridiculous–rising to outright defiance with the kitten dolls that flaunt their sexless sassy behinds–may sit well with a talent for survival, turning energies of derision around and using them to ride out a bad moment. Make no mistake, Phelan's doll drawings are all moments to be ridden out, lived through, undergone. To resist their psychological tug may be to cast oneself as a stuckup connoisseur doll or an uptight bourgeois doll or something else delectably idiotic and, come to think of it, perhaps kind of interesting.

Of course the drawings are beautiful. They are high-art bravura beautiful, the work of an artist justly celebrated (most tellingly, by other painters) for majestic, all but imageless paintings gracefully and gravely refined in sensibility. Phelan is as serious about art as anyone else I know, and it does not surprise her friends that she has often expressed a certain alarm at finding herself drawn into work that is, among other things, such *fun*. Here perhaps is a metajoke–Aesthete Ellen, caught playing with dolls—underlying the local jokes of the drawings. The happiness of it is the way Phelan's talent reacts to playing hookie from high endeavor. Her talent sings. With ravishing specificities of tone and texture, it transforms an idea that at first blush seems intrinsically illustrational into something mildly unprecedented, a species of still life

XIV. *Bud Man*, 1987

tion of continuity in art's traditional means and ends. An artist marks up a piece of paper, and that's art. No problem. Is this airy suggestion over-simple? In the charmed aura of the doll drawings, it is not simple at all unless miracles are simple.

For a moment in that Avis office, I was crazy about the woman who was looking daggers at me. Her blushing energy was terrifically attractive, as the daggers bounced off my innocence. The jerk she took me for would have said, "You're beautiful when you're angry." Fortunately, I was speechless. The man I had talked to on the phone came forward with the lost doll. I saw the woman realize her mistake and relax her hostility—*mistaken again*. I returned to the car and my weeping child, whose gratitude at recovering her pretend baby made me feel how lovely it is to be a daddy. Our nuclear family tooled off into the L.A. night— "Down Life's Highway," to borrow the title of Ellen Phelan's dazzling mouse-ification of weddedness. I know that road. It is unbeatable for going places, but it can lay some heavy distractions on your sense of what you are.

crossed with figuration, cartooning taking an oath of naturalism, realism as chatty with poetic tales as the Ancient Mariner.

There is nothing else in art exactly like Phelan's doll series, though no end of things that are *almost* like it. Stylistically, the series is a prism catching glints of affinity with everything from Watteau and Fuseli to the work of innumerable contemporaries—and those contemporaries as variegated as the synthetic-naturalist Eric Fischl and the cartoon-wielding trickster Steve Gianankos. Indeed, the doll drawings somewhat resemble so much other art that they can end up seeming to resemble art in general, as if hitting on some primitive square-root theorem that qualifies something as art instead of as something else. In the context of a present art world bedeviled by uncertainty about what art is and what artists do, the upshot is altogether affirmative, a refreshing and reassuring demonstra-

IX. *Down Life's Highway*, 1986

V. *Beth and the Poet*, 1985

XVI. *Mother and Daughter (Esmeralda)*, 1987

XXIII. *Good Time Charlie*, 1988

XV. *Fireman and Snowman*, 1987

XXVIII. *Self as Elf*, 1989

XXXVIII. *Street Scene: A Memory of Detroit*, 1991

EXHIBITION CHECKLIST

All dimensions indicate image size. Height precedes width.

DRAWINGS

I. *Applause*, 1985
Gouache on paper
22 1/2 x 19 1/2"
Collection Susanne Feld Hilberry
and Richard Kandarian,
Birmingham, Michigan

II. *Baby and Pierre*, 1985
Gouache on paper
20 1/2 x 14 1/4"
Private Collection, Courtesy Thea
Westreich, New York

III. *Baby and Old Man*, 1985
Gouache on paper
22 1/2 x 15"
Collection Mr. and Mrs. Peter Frank,
Montclair, New Jersey

IV. *Beth and Amy*, 1985
Gouache on paper
22 1/4 x 18 1/4"
Collection Raymond J. Learsy,
New York

V. *Beth and the Poet*, 1985
Gouache on paper
20 1/2 x 14 1/2"
Collection Eric Fischl, New York

VI. *Old Man II*, 1985
Gouache on paper
15 1/4 x 16 1/2"
Collection Ross Bleckner, New York

VII. *A Shock (Oh-Oh)*, 1986
Gouache on paper
20 1/2 x 13 1/2"
Collection David Wirtz, New York

VIII. *Beth as Diva*, 1986
Gouache on paper
19 1/2 x 12 1/2"
Collection of the artist

IX. *Down Life's Highway*, 1986
Gouache on paper
20 x 16"
Collection Jean C. Pigozzi, New York

X. *Rejecting Mother*, 1986
Gouache on paper
19 1/2 x 20 1/2"
Collection of the artist

XI. *Spectre of Age*, 1986
Gouache on paper
13 1/2 x 11"
Collection of the artist

XII. *Bride of Despair*, 1987
Watercolor on paper
10 7/8 x 7 3/4"
Courtesy Barbara Toll Fine Arts,
New York

XIII. *Bride of Fashion*, 1987
Watercolor on paper
7 3/8 x 7 5/8"
Courtesy Barbara Toll Fine Arts,
New York

XIV. *Bud Man*, 1987
Gouache and watercolor on paper
33 1/2 x 20 1/2"
Collection H. David Zucca,
Ann Arbor, Michigan

XV. *Fireman and Snowman*, 1987
Watercolor on paper
19 3/4 x 19 1/4"
Collection Michael and Judy Ovitz,
Los Angeles

XVI. *Mother and Daughter (Esmeralda)*,
1987
Gouache on paper
26 7/8 x 17 1/2"
Collection Mr. and Mrs. John O'Neill,
Birmingham, Michigan

XVII. *Mother and Daughter (The
Presentation)*, 1987
Gouache on paper
28 x 19 5/8"
Collection Irwin and Judith Elson,
Bloomfield Hills, Michigan

XVIII. *Mug Shot*, 1987
Watercolor on paper
15 1/2 x 30"
Collection Jeffrey Slatkin,
Birmingham, Michigan

XIX. *Traveling Costume*, 1987
Watercolor on paper
20 x 18 3/4"
Collection Joel Shapiro

XX. *Whose Future?*, 1987
Watercolor and gouache on paper
13 x 10"
Collection Barbara Toll, New York

XXI. *Witness*, 1987
Gouache and watercolor on paper
17 1/2 x 13 7/8"
Collection Elizabeth Murray,
New York

XXII. *Bride and Groom*, 1988
Watercolor on paper
13 3/4 x 10 1/4"
Courtesy Barbara Toll Fine Arts,
New York

XXIII. *Good Time Charlie*, 1988
Gouache on paper
28 1/2 x 20 1/4"
Collection Freddy and Candy DeMann,
Los Angeles

XXIV. *Matinee Idol*, 1988
Watercolor on paper
29 x 21"
Private collection

XXV. *Minstrel Show (Dancer)*, 1988
Watercolor on paper
21 1/4 x 29"
Collection Dr. Jack E. Chachkes,
New York

XXVI. *Singer, study for "Applause"*, 1988
Gouache on paper
12 x 8 5/8"
Collection Irene Worth, New York

XXVII. *Wrestlers*, 1988
Watercolor on paper
21 $^1/_4$ x 20 $^3/_4$"
Courtesy Asher/Faure, Los Angeles

XXVIII. *Self as Elf*, 1989
Gouache on paper
31 $^1/_8$ x 23 $^5/_8$"
Collection Ann Ehrenkrantz,
New York

XXIX. *In the Shadows*, 1990
Watercolor on paper
21 x 18 $^1/_4$"
Courtesy Barbara Toll Fine Arts,
New York

XXX. *A Word of Advice*, 1991
Watercolor on paper
28 $^3/_8$ x 20 $^7/_8$"
Courtesy Barbara Toll Fine Arts,
New York

XXXI. *Baby, Horse and Mirror*, 1991
Gouache on paper
21 x 28 $^1/_2$"
Private Collection

XXXII. *Blonde White Woman #4*, 1991
Watercolor on paper
20 x 19 $^3/_8$"
Courtesy Barbara Toll Fine Arts,
New York

XXXIII. *Blonde White Woman #9*, 1991
Watercolor on paper
20 $^1/_4$ x 19 $^{15}/_{16}$"
Courtesy Barbara Toll Fine Arts,
New York

XXXIV. *Family*, 1991
Watercolor on paper
21 x 29 $^1/_2$"
Collection Dr. and Mrs. Martin Weissman,
Michigan

XXXV. *Mama*, 1991
Gouache on paper
20 x 17 $^1/_4$"
Courtesy Barbara Toll Fine Arts,
New York

XXXVI. *On the Avenue*, 1991
Watercolor on paper
29 x 21 $^1/_2$"
Courtesy Asher/Faure, Los Angeles

XXXVII. *Rehearsal*, 1991
Watercolor on paper
25 $^1/_4$ x 39 $^1/_4$"
Collection Dr. and Mrs. Gordon M. Moss,
Southfield, Michigan

XXXVIII. *Street Scene: A Memory of Detroit*, 1991
Gouache on paper
19 $^7/_8$ x 19 $^1/_4$"
Collection Bruce and Judith Eissner

XXXIX. *The Kiss: Betrayal*, 1991
Watercolor and gouache on paper
21 $^1/_2$ x 29 $^1/_8$"
Collection Mr. and Mrs. Eric Lieber,
Beverly Hills, California

XL. *The Kiss: Revenge*, 1991
Watercolor and gouache on paper
20 $^1/_8$ x 28 $^1/_2$"
Courtesy Susanne Hilberry Gallery,
Birmingham, Michigan

XLI. *War: Sailor and Barmaid*, 1991
Watercolor on paper
19 $^3/_4$ x 19 $^3/_4$"
Private collection

PAINTINGS

XLII. *Baby and Pierre (Run Baby)*, 1991
Oil on linen
29 x 22"
Collection Susanne Feld Hilberry and
Richard Kandarian, Birmingham,
Michigan

XLIII. *My Brother Imagined as My Sister*, 1991
Oil on linen
33 $^3/_8$ x 27 $^3/_8$"
Courtesy Barbara Toll Fine Arts,
New York

XLIV. *Overheard: the Conversation*, 1991
Oil on linen
41 $^1/_2$ x 58 $^7/_8$"
Courtesy Barbara Toll Fine Arts,
New York

XLV. *Rehearsal*, 1991
Oil on linen
41 x 64 $^1/_4$"
Collection Dr. and Mrs. Martin
Weissman, Michigan

XLVI. *Rejecting Mother*, 1991
Oil on linen
29 $^1/_4$ x 33 $^3/_4$"
Courtesy Susanne Hilberry Gallery,
Birmingham, Michigan

XLVII. *Baby, Horse and Mirror*, 1992
Oil on linen
42 $^1/_8$ x 56 $^1/_8$"
Courtesy Barbara Toll Fine Arts,
New York

XLVIII. *Beth and the Poet*, 1992
Oil on linen
43 $^1/_2$ x 31 $^1/_2$"
Courtesy Barbara Toll Fine Arts,
New York

XLIX. *Matinee Idol*, 1992
Oil on linen
43 $^1/_2$ x 31 $^3/_4$"
Courtesy Barbara Toll Fine Arts,
New York

L. *The Beautiful Mother*, 1992
Oil on linen
29 x 33 $^3/_4$"
Courtesy Barbara Toll Fine Arts,
New York

LI. *The Kiss: Betrayal*, 1992
Oil on linen
43 x 58 $^1/_4$"
Courtesy Barbara Toll Fine Arts,
New York

LII. *Street Scene: Memory of Detroit (for Joyce Carol Oates)*, 1992
Oil on linen
39 $^3/_4$ x 38 $^1/_2$"
Courtesy Barbara Toll Fine Arts,
New York

BIOGRAPHY

Ellen Phelan

Born in Detroit, Michigan, 1943
Lives and works in New York City and Westport, New York

Education

1969   Bachelor of Fine Arts, Wayne State University, Detroit

1971   Master of Fine Arts, Wayne State University, Detroit

Selected One-Person Exhibitions

1972   *Ellen Phelan*, Willis Gallery, Detroit

1974   *Ellen Phelan*, Willis Gallery, Detroit

1975   *Ellen Phelan*, Artists Space, New York

1977   *Watercolors*, Susanne Hilberry Gallery, Birmingham, Michigan

1979   *Ellen Phelan: Matrix #48*, (curated by Edward Albee) Wadsworth Atheneum, Hartford (with exhibition brochure)

Paintings and Constructions, Susanne Hilberry Gallery, Birmingham, Michigan

1-2-3-4 Smaller Paintings, Ruth Schaffner Gallery, Los Angeles

1980   *Paintings*, The Clocktower, The Institute for Art and Urban Resources, New York

Paintings, Hansen-Fuller-Goldeen Gallery, San Francisco

1981   *New Paintings*, Susanne Hilberry Gallery, Birmingham, Michigan

Paintings and Drawings from 1977-1981, Dart Gallery, Chicago

1982   *Ellen Phelan*, Hansen-Fuller-Goldeen Gallery, San Francisco

New Paintings, Susanne Hilberry Gallery, Birmingham, Michigan

Paintings, Barbara Toll Fine Arts, New York

1984   *Paintings: 1979-1984*, Susanne Hilberry Gallery, Birmingham, Michigan

1985   *Ellen Phelan: New Works*, Barbara Toll Fine Arts, New York

1986   *Paintings*, Susanne Hilberry Gallery, Birmingham, Michigan

Ellen Phelan–Paintings, Barbara Toll Fine Arts, New York

1987   *DOLLS: watercolors/gouaches*, Barbara Toll Fine Arts, New York

1988   *DOLLS*, Susanne Hilberry Gallery, Birmingham, Michigan

1989   *Landscapes*, Barbara Toll Fine Arts, New York

Ellen Phelan, Asher/Faure, Los Angeles

Drawing Now: Ellen Phelan, The Baltimore Museum of Art, Maryland (with exhibition brochure)

1990   *Ellen Phelan: Paintings*, Susanne Hilberry Gallery, Birmingham, Michigan

Recent Work, Barbara Toll Fine Arts, New York

1991   *Ellen Phelan*, Members' Gallery, Albright-Knox Art Gallery, Buffalo

1992   *Ellen Phelan: Doll Drawings*, Asher/Faure, Los Angeles

Doll Paintings, Barbara Toll Fine Arts, New York

Dolls, Susanne Hilberry Gallery, Birmingham, Michigan

Ellen Phelan: From the Lives of Dolls, (curated by Marge Goldwater) University Gallery, University of Massachusetts, Amherst (with exhibition catalogue)

Selected Group Exhibitions

1970   *58th Exhibition for Michigan Artists*, The Detroit Institute of Arts

1971   *Jim Chatelain, Nancy Mitchnick, Ellen Phelan*, Willis Gallery, Detroit

1972   *Women Artists' Recent Work*, J.L. Hudson Gallery, Detroit

Critics Selection from Detroit Galleries, (organized by Sam Hunter) Cranbrook Academy of Art Museum, Bloomfield Hills, Michigan

1974 *Michigan Focus/Works on Paper*, Grand Rapids Art Museum, Grand Rapids, Michigan

1975 *Spring Group Exhibition*, Paula Cooper Gallery, New York

1976 *Paintings*, (organized by Annina Nosei) Fine Arts Building, New York

Group Show, Paula Cooper Gallery, New York

Soho, (organized by Paula Cooper) Akademie der Kunste, West Berlin, Germany

Opening Exhibition, Susanne Hilberry Gallery, Birmingham, Michigan

1977 *Ellen Phelan/Jeremy Gilbert-Rolfe*, Paula Cooper Gallery, New York

Abstract Images, Willard Gallery, New York

Spectrum '77: Painting & Sculpture, Charlotte Crosby Kemper Gallery, Kansas City Art Institute, Kansas City, Missouri

New York, (organized by Julian Pretto) N.A.M.E. Gallery, Chicago

New Abstract Objects, Hallwalls Contemporary Arts Center, Buffalo

1978 *Art is for the Spirit*, Paula Cooper Gallery, New York

1979 *Pittura Ambiente*, (organized by Francesca Alinova) Palazzo Reale, Milan, Italy (with exhibition catalogue)

Drawing, Paula Cooper Gallery, New York

Willis Revisited, Willis Gallery, Detroit

At Cranbrook, Downtown Detroit, 21 Artists, Cranbrook Academy of Art Museum, Bloomfield Hills, Michigan (with exhibition catalogue)

Art on Paper–1979, Weatherspoon Art Gallery, University of North Carolina, Greensboro

Drawings, Members' Gallery, Albright-Knox Art Gallery, Buffalo

1980 *Invitational*, David Winton Bell Gallery, List Art Center, Brown University, Providence, Rhode Island

Contemporary American Painting, (organized by Richard Armstrong) Lake Placid Center for the Arts, XIII Olympic Winter Games, Lake Placid, New York

Painted Structures, Jeffrey Fuller Fine Arts Ltd., Philadelphia

Drawings of a Different Nature, (organized by Lynda Benglis) Portland Center for the Visual Arts, Portland, Oregon

Summer/80, The Drawing Center, New York

Paintings By, Brooke Alexander Gallery, New York

Kick Out the Jams: Detroit's Cass Corridor 1963-1977, Detroit Institute of Arts; traveled to the Museum of Contemporary Art, Chicago (with exhibition catalogue)

3-Dimensional Painting, (curated by Judith Tannenbaum) Museum of Contemporary Art, Chicago (with exhibition catalogue)

1981 *Watercolors*, (curated by Brooks Adams) P.S.1 Museum, The Institute for Art and Urban Resources, Long Island City, New York

Ellen Phelan and David Strome, Art Latitude Gallery, New York

1982 *New Drawing in America*, The Drawing Center, New York; traveled to Sutton Place, Guildford, Surrey, England, and Gallerie d'Arte Moderna di Ca'Pesaro, Venice, Italy

American Abstraction Now, The Institute of Contemporary Art of the Virginia Museum, Richmond, Virginia

Amerikanische Zeichnungen, Galerie Biedermann, Munich, Germany

1983 *Alternative Approaches to Landscape*, Thomas Segal Gallery, Boston

Landscape, Ben Shahn Galleries, William Paterson College, Wayne, New Jersey

Terminal–New York, (organized by Frederick Ted Castle) Harborside Industrial Center, Brooklyn

1984 *Nature as Image*, Organization of Independent Artists, New York

1+1=2, (curated by Bernice Steinbaum and Paul Brach) Bernice Steinbaum Gallery, New York; traveled to Brentwood Gallery, St. Louis; Irvine Fine Art Gallery, University of California, Irvine; Gallery of Art, University of Northern Iowa, Cedar Falls, Iowa (with exhibition catalogue)

New Vistas: Contemporary American Landscape, The Hudson River Museum of Westchester, Yonkers (with exhibition catalogue)

Viewpoint 84, Out of Square, Cranbrook Academy of Art Museum, Bloomfield Hills, Michigan (with exhibition brochure)

Three Painters: Hermine Ford, Jan Hashey & Ellen Phelan, Barbara Toll Fine Arts, New York

Cross Portraits, Detroit Focus Gallery, Detroit

A Decade of Artists Space, Artists Space, New York

Landscape, Matthews Hamilton Gallery, Philadelphia

Works on Paper, Barbara Krakow Gallery, Boston

SEX, Cable Gallery, New York

Drawings, Barbara Toll Fine Arts, New York

1985 *Painting–1985*, Pam Adler Gallery, New York

Group Show, Susanne Hilberry Gallery, Birmingham, Michigan

Drawings, Knight Gallery, Spirit Square Center for the Arts, Charlotte, North Carolina

Drawings: 1975-1985, Barbara Toll Fine Arts, New York

1986 *Drawings: 60's to the 80's*, Barbara Toll Fine Arts, New York

1987 *The New Romantic Landscape*, Whitney Museum of American Art, Fairfield County, Stamford, Connecticut (with exhibition brochure)

Objects, Barbara Toll Fine Arts, New York

Solid Abstraction, Saxon-Lee Gallery, Los Angeles

Contemporary American Art: Selections from the Edward R. Downe, Jr. Collection, (curated by Klaus Kertess) The Parrish Art Museum, Southampton, New York

1988 *Works on Paper*, Curt Marcus Gallery, New York

Of Another Nature, Loughelton Gallery, New York (with exhibition catalogue)

Recent Drawings: George Condo, Mike Kelley, Ellen Phelan, Janice Provisor, Whitney Museum of American Art, New York (with exhibition brochure)

1989 *100 Drawings by Women*, Hillwood Art Museum, Long Island University, C.W. Post Campus, Brookville, New York

Epiphanies, Edward Thorp Gallery, New York

Scale, Space, Structure, Ben Shahn Galleries, William Paterson College, Wayne, New Jersey

A Decade of American Drawing 1980–1989, Daniel Weinberg Gallery, Los Angeles

Topography, Fuller Gross Gallery, San Francisco

The Eighties in Review: Selections from the Permanent Collection, Whitney Museum of American Art, Fairfield County, Stamford, Connecticut (with exhibition brochure)

Drawings from the Eighties from the Collection, The Museum of Modern Art, New York

Writ in Water, Solo Press/Solo Gallery, New York

Underneath It All, Maxwell Davidson Gallery, New York

1990 *Terra Incognita–New Directions in Contemporary Landscape*, Museum of Art, Rhode Island School of Design, Providence

Re:Framing Cartoons: In and Out of Context, (curated by Tom Zummer) Loughelton Gallery, New York

Drawings, Paula Cooper Gallery, New York

Landscapes on Paper, Graham Modern, New York

Minimalism and Post-Minimalism: Drawing Distinctions, Hood Museum of Art, Dartmouth College, Hanover, New Hampshire; traveled to The Parrish Art Museum, Southampton, New York (with exhibition catalogue)

1991 *Invitational*, The New Britain Museum of American Art, New Britain, Connecticut (with exhibition catalogue)

Drawings, Susanne Hilberry Gallery, Birmingham, Michigan

Not on Canvas, Asher/Faure, Los Angeles

Landscape Paintings, Annina Nosei Gallery, New York

1991 Biennial Exhibition, Whitney Museum of American Art, New York (with exhibition catalogue)

Landscape: Seven Views, Nina Freudenheim Gallery, Buffalo

Watercolor Across the Ages with Selected 20th Century American Works, The Gallery at Bristol-Myers Squibb, Princeton, New Jersey (with exhibition catalogue)

1992 *Allegories of Modernism: Contemporary Drawing*, The Museum of Modern Art, New York (with exhibition catalogue)

Vision Quest, Cleveland State University Art Gallery, Cleveland, Ohio

Drawn in the Nineties, (curated by Joshua P. Smith) co-sponsored by the Katonah Museum of Art, Katonah, New York and Independent Curators Incorporated, New York; traveling to the Fine Arts Gallery, Indiana University, Bloomington; Illingworth Kerr Gallery, Calgary, Alberta, Canada; and the Huntsville Museum of Art, Huntsville, Alabama (with exhibition catalogue)

Slow Art: Painting in New York Now, P.S.1 Museum, The Institute for Contemporary Art, Long Island City, New York

Re:Framing Cartoons, (curated by Tom Zummer) Wexner Center for the Arts, Ohio State University, Columbus (with exhibition catalogue)

Earth and Sky: Recent Paintings by Katherine Bowling, Joan Nelson, and Ellen Phelan, Hood Museum of Art, Dartmouth College, Hanover, New Hampshire (with exhibition brochure)

Selected Bibliography

1976

Pozzi, Lucio. "Questa Nuova Tendenza e di Grande Rilievo." *Bolaffiarte*, May-June, pp. 47-53.

Schwartz, Barbara. "Ellen Phelan at Artists Space Gallery." Review, *Craft Horizons*, April, p. 18.

1977

Lubell, Ellen. "Jeremy Gilbert-Rolfe/Ellen Phelan." Review, *ARTS Magazine*, April, pp. 36-37.

Shapiro, Lindsay Stamm. "Ellen Phelan at Paula Cooper." Review, *Craft Horizons*, April, p. 53.

Wooster, Ann-Sargent. "Ellen Phelan (Paula Cooper)." Review, *ARTnews*, April, p. 129.

1979

At Cranbrook, Downtown Detroit, 21 Artists. Exhibition catalogue; introduction by Roy Slade. Bloomfield Hills, Michigan: Cranbrook Academy of Art Museum.

Ellen Phelan: Matrix 48. Exhibition brochure; essay by Edward Albee. Hartford, Connecticut: Wadsworth Atheneum.

Pittura Ambiente. Exhibition catalogue; essays by Francesca Alinova and Renato Barilli, Palazzo Reale, Milan. Milan, Italy: Comune di Milano; Ripartisione cultura.

1980

3-Dimensional Painting. Exhibition catalogue; essay by Judith Tannenbaum. Chicago, Illinois: Museum of Contemporary Art.

Carlson, Prudence. "Ellen Phelan at The Clocktower." Review, *Art in America*, May, pp. 155-156.

Kick Out the Jams: Detroit's Cass Corridor 1963-1977. Exhibition catalogue; essays by Jay Belloli and Mary Jane Jacob. Detroit, Michigan: The Detroit Institute of Arts.

1981

Armstrong, Richard. "Ellen Phelan, Dart Gallery." Review, *ARTFORUM*, October, p. 83.

Kahn, Barry. "John Egner & Ellen Phelan: Reconstructing the Jams." *New Art Examiner*, June, pp. 6-7.

1982

Armstrong, Richard. "Report from Detroit: Was Cass Corridor a Style?" *Art in America*, February, pp. 34-39.

_____. "Un Tour d'horizon - Mary Heilmann and Ellen Phelan." *BOMB Magazine*, 1982, no.4, pp. 14-15.

Kahn, Barry. "Content Without Representation?" *Monthly Detroit*, February, pp. 29-32.

1983

Jayne, Kristie. "Ellen Phelan." Review, *ARTS Magazine*, January, p. 33.

1984

1+1=2. Exhibition catalogue; essays by Donald Kuspit and Melinda Wortz. New York: Bernice Steinbaum Gallery.

New Vistas: Contemporary American Landscape. Exhibition catalogue; essay by Janice C. Oresman. Yonkers, New York: The Hudson River Museum of Westchester.

SELECTIONS: From the BankAmerica Corporation Art Collection. Brochure for Bank of America Plaza, New York, essay by Bonnie-Earls Solari, San Francisco.

Viewpoint 84, Out of Square. Exhibition brochure; introduction by Roy Slade and essay by George Ortman. Bloomfield Hills, Michigan: Cranbrook Academy of Art Museum.

1985

Futtner, Joseph. "Ellen Phelan." Review, *ARTS Magazine*, September, p. 4 .

Madoff, Steven Henry. "Ellen Phelan." Review, *ARTnews*, October, pp. 133-134.

Westfall, Stephen. "Ellen Phelan at Barbara Toll." Review, *Art in America*, September, p. 133.

Whitehead Institute Art Collection. Catalogue of the collection; forward by David Baltimore and introduction by Stephen Johnson and Lucille Aptekar. Cambridge, Massachusetts: Whitehead Institute for Biomedical Research.

1986

Barron, John. "Phelan's Paintings after Paintings." *Detroit Monthly*, May, p. 132.

Carducci, Vincent A. "Ellen Phelan, Susanne Hilberry Gallery." Review, *New Art Examiner*, June pp. 53-54.

Madoff, Steven Henry. "The Return of Abstraction." *ARTnews*, January, pp. 80-85.

Russell, John. "Ellen Phelan at Barbara Toll." Review, *The New York Times*, November 21, p. C25.

1987

Gill, Susan. "Ellen Phelan." Review, *ARTnews*, February, p. 137.

Gimelson, Deborah. "Talk of The Trade: X-mas X-tras." *Art & Auction*, December, p. 46.

Loughery, John. "Ellen Phelan." Review, *ARTS Magazine*, January, pp. 125-126.

_____. "The New Romantic Landscape." Review, *ARTS Magazine*, November, p. 107.

The New Romantic Landscape. Exhibition brochure; essays by Chantal Combes and Peter Doroshenko. Stamford, Connecticut: Whitney Museum of American Art, Fairfield County.

Spector, Buzz. "Ellen Phelan, Barbara Toll Fine Arts." Review, *ARTFORUM*, February, pp. 113-114.

1988

Henry, Gerrit. "Ellen Phelan: The Interpretation of Dolls." *Print Collector's Newsletter*, May-June, pp. 51-53.

Of Another Nature. Exhibition catalogue; essays by Frank Gillette, Steven Harvey and Amy Lipton. New York: Loughelton Gallery.

Johnson, Ken. "Ellen Phelan at Barbara Toll." Review, *Art in America*, March, p. 151.

Loughery, John. "Landscape Painting in The Eighties: April Gornik, Ellen Phelan and Joan Nelson." *ARTS Magazine*, May, pp. 44-48.

Recent Drawings: George Condo, Mike Kelley, Ellen Phelan, Janice Provisor. Exhibition brochure; introduction by Richard Armstrong, essay by Roni Feinstein. New York: Whitney Museum of American Art.

Westfall, Stephen. "Ellen Phelan, Barbara Toll." Review, *Flash Art*, March-April, pp. 114-115.

1989

The Eighties in Review: Selections from the Permanent Collection. Exhibition brochure; essay by Roni Feinstein. Stamford, Connecticut: Whitney Museum of American Art, Fairfield County.

Adams, Brooks. "Ellen Phelan at Barbara Toll." Review, *Art in America*, November, p. 192.

Drawing Now: Ellen Phelan. Exhibition brochure; essay by Jan Howard. Baltimore, Maryland: The Baltimore Museum of Art.

Liebmann, Lisa. "Studio Visits." *Mirabella*, July, p. 75.

Solnit, Rebecca. "Landscape As Cultural Solution." *Artweek*, September 23, p. 6.

Wilbert, Robert. "Interview: Ellen Phelan." *Detroit Focus Quarterly*, Winter, pp. 3-5, 13.

1990

Brody, Jacqueline. "Ellen Phelan." Prints & Photographs Published, *Print Collector's Newsletter*, May-June, p. 62.

Minimalism and Post-Minimalism: Drawing Distinctions. Exhibition catalogue. Hanover, New Hampshire: Hood Museum of Art, Dartmouth College.

Pagel, David. "Ellen Phelan." *Art Issues*, February.

1991

1991 Biennial Exhibition. Exhibition catalogue; essays by Richard Armstrong, Lisa Phillips and Richard Marshall. New York: Whitney Museum of American Art.

1991 Invitational. Exhibition catalogue; essay by Janice La Motta. New Britain, Connecticut: New Britain Museum of American Art.

Brody, Jacqueline, ed. "Ellen Phelan." Prints & Photographs Published, *Print Collector's Newsletter*, January-February, p. 231.

Watercolor Across the Ages with Selected 20th Century American Works. Exhibition catalogue; essay by Ronny Cohen. Princeton, New Jersey: The Gallery at Bristol-Myers Squibb.

1992

Allegories of Modernism: Contemporary Drawing. Exhibition catalogue; essay by Bernice Rose. New York: The Museum of Modern Art (distributed by Harry N. Abrams Inc.).

Baker, Kenneth. "New York: Allegories of Modernism." *Artspace*, July/August, pp. 62-63.

Drawn in the Nineties. Exhibition catalogue; introduction by Joshua P. Smith and essay by Sean Rainbird. New York: co-sponsored by the Katonah Museum of Art and Independent Curators Incorporated.

Drucker, Johanna. "Visual Pleasure: A Feminist Perspective." M/E/A/N/I/N/G, May, pp. 3-11

Earth and Sky: Recent Paintings by Katherine Bowling, Joan Nelson, and Ellen Phelan. Exhibition brochure; introduction and essays by Katherine Merrill. Hanover, New Hampshire: Hood Museum of Art, Dartmouth College.

Ellen Phelan: From the Lives of Dolls. Exhibition catalogue; essays by Richard Armstrong and Peter Schjeldahl. Amherst, Massachusetts: University Gallery, University of Massachusetts.

Moorman, Margaret. "Ellen Phelan: Shapechanger." *ARTnews*, February, pp.108-113.

Perl, Jed. "so surreal." *Vogue*, August, pp. 132-136.

Re:Framing Cartoons. Exhibition catalogue; essay by Tom Zummer. Columbus, Ohio: Wexner Center for the Arts, Ohio State University.

Schjeldahl, Peter. "Drawing Blood." *The Village Voice*, March 3, p. 85.

Weissman, Benjamin. "Ellen Phelan: Asher/Faure." Review, *Artforum*, March, p. 115.